Welcome to the galaxy of New South Wales Year 3 handwriting!

Hello, my name is Sirius, and I am the brightest star in the night sky! I'm here to help you along the way ... in a *Sirius* kind of way!

My ticket to the Moon

Name: _____

Age: _____ Class: _____

Birthday: _____

Teacher: _____

My progress passport

You are travelling on a spaceship expedition around the galaxy. Colour in the circles as you progress through the book.

Start here

Passport

f
I can write a head, body and tail letter.

Aa
I can print.

ig
I can do drop-in joins.

if
I can drop in the letter f.

na
I can connect drop-in joins to a, c, d, g, o and q.

oc
I remember to retrace for horizontal joins to anti-clockwise letters.

oh
I can retrace horizontal joins to tall letters.

ff
I can do horizontal joins to double letters.

OXFORD UNIVERSITY PR

Good work! Keep going!

a l
I can add exit flicks to letters.

m
I can add entry flicks.

qu
I can make a diagonal join from q to u.

ze
I know z has a little wave at the base.

hi
I can do diagonal joins.

on
an do horizontal joins.

bg
I know the letters b, g, j, p, s and y do not join.

AB
I remember capital letters do not join.

Blast off!
I can write fluently and legibly.

Before you begin writing ...

Here are the **3Ps** that will help you with your writing: **p**osture, **p**encil grip and **p**aper position. You will be reminded about these as you go through the book.

Posture

Relax your arms and make sure the chair supports your back. Put your feet flat on the floor.

Pencil grip

One of the most important decisions you can make is how you hold your pencil. Hold your pencil firmly between your thumb and index finger, balanced on your middle finger. (Your grip should be 2.5 centimetres before the end of the pencil. Don't grip too tightly!)

Left-handed

Right-handed

Paper position

Angle your page and use your non-writing hand to steady the page.

Left-handed

Right-handed

Tip!

Left-handers may form some letters differently. For example, for the capital letters A, E, F, H and T, the left-handed person might go from right to left to make the join.

OXFORD UNIVERSITY PRE

NSW Foundation Style print

Printing letters

Learning intention:
To revise NSW Foundation Style
print handwriting

Trace these lower-case and capital letters.

aA   bB   cC   dD   eE   fF   gG

hH   iI   jJ   kK   lL   mM   nN

oO   pP   qQ   rR   sS   tT   uU

vV   wW   xX   yY   zZ

Find and print all the tall lower-case letters that touch the dotted line as shown.

above
on   f h
below

Find and print all the short lower-case letters.

above
on   a c
below

above
on
below

Find and print all the tail lower-case letters.

above
on   g j
below

Printing numerals

Trace and then copy these numerals.

1 1 1   6 6 6

2 2 2   7 7 7

3 3 3   8 8 8

4 4 4   9 9 9

5 5 5   10 10 10

Printing punctuation

Trace and then copy these punctuation marks on the lines as shown.

! ! !

, , ,

; ; ;

? ? ?   " "   / / /

Printing names

ip! When we label maps and diagrams, we use print handwriting.

Neptune   Saturn

Venus   Uranus

Mars   Earth

Jupiter   Mercury

"**M**y **V**ery **E**ducated **M**other **J**ust **S**erved **U**s **N**oodles"

Match the name of the planet to the correct image and write it in the box in print handwriting.

_____

_____

_____

_____

_____

_____

_____

_____

Direction of movement

Clockwise movements

Trace and then copy these clockwise patterns.

Clockwise

Trace and then copy these clockwise letters.

m   n   r   h

b   p   k

Complete the numbers on the clock. Then complete the grey line around the clock and add an arrow to show which way is clockwise.

What time is showing on this clock?

DID YOU KNOW ...
that a day on Saturn is only 11 hours?

Anti-clockwise movements

Trace and then copy these anti-clockwise patterns.

Anti-clockwise

Trace and then copy the anti-clockwise letters.

a   c   d   e   f

g   o   q   s

Write each anti-clockwise letter in the correct column. Write its capital letter next to it.

Short letters	Tall and tail letters
aA	gG

Downstroke and straight-line patterns

Learning intention:

To practise letters that have a straight line

Trace and then copy these downstroke movements.

Trace and then copy these horizontal movements.

Trace and then copy these downstroke letters.

l   i   t   h   j   f

Diagonal letters

Trace and then copy these diagonal movements. Start at the dot.

Trace and then copy these combined movements.

Trace and then copy these diagonal lower-case letters and capital letters.

Trace the diagonal track of the shooting stars, using the dot as a starting point.

Consolidating

Learning intention: To practise more patterns before writing

Trace and then copy.

Assessment: Print handwriting

Write all the capital and lower-case letters of the alphabet in print handwriting.

Aa   Bb

Copy the following in print handwriting.

A day on Mercury is 1408 hours and on

Venus it is 5832 hours. A day on Earth

is 24 hours and on Mars it is 25 hours.

Self-assessment of print handwriting:

Congratulations! You have learnt how to print. Colour in your progress on page 2.

 ❏ I need more confidence

 ❏ I understand but need practice

 ❏ Over the Moon!

Teacher comment

Passport

Exit flicks

Learning intention:

To add exit flicks to help get from one letter to another

Introducing exit flicks

What is an exit flick?

Tip! Exit flicks help you get from one letter to another when joining letters in a word.

The letter a starts like this.

Then we add an exit flick.

$a \rightarrow a$

Trace these letters with exit flicks.

a d h k m n u i l t o v w

Trace these letters and words. Add the missing letters to complete the word. Note! One is a capital letter.

a a a	s t e r o i d s
d d d	_ w a r f p l a n e t
o o o	t e c h n _ l _ g y
v v v	g r a _ i t y
h h h	g r e e n _ o u s e
k k k	_ u i p e r b e l t
m m m	_ e t e o r
n n n	s u p e r _ o v a
w w w	_ h i t e d _ a r f

OXFORD UNIVERSITY PRES

Practising exit flicks

Wow! You are really good at this skill!

I am successful when I can:

❏ check my 3Ps
❏ make my exit flick smooth rather than pointy.

Trace and then copy.

There are thousands and thousands

of asteroids. Most asteroids are

located between Mars and Jupiter.

This is called the asteroid belt.

Small, rocky asteroids orbit the Sun.

Self-assessment   Draw a star on three of your smoothest exit flicks.

Letters without exit flicks

Tip! Capital letters do not have an exit flick because they don't join to other letters.

Trace and then copy.

Claudia and Ali went on a mission to

Jupiter, the fifth planet from the Sun.

They also visited Mars, Saturn, Uranus

and Neptune on their mission.

They also saw asteroids and comets.

Letters that change: f

The f changes from this ____f____ to this: ____f____ .

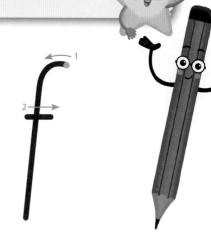

Tip! You will notice that the letter f now adds a tail below the baseline.

Trace these letters.

f   f   f   f   f   f   f

Trace and then copy.

full   face   fine   family

friends   fire   find   first

focus   fusion

I feel strong holding this full Moon and now knowing how to write the letter f.

Passport

Consolidating

Trace and then copy.

Sirius and Juliette loved travelling to

space in a rocket. The absence of gravity

made them feel as light as a feather. It was

like floating through a mystical, untouched

world. (Gravity is a force that holds you

to Earth's surface.) For years it was

believed that Earth was the only planet

in our solar system with liquid water.

Recently, NASA revealed that there is

intermittent running water on Mars too.

There are more stars in the universe than

grains of sand on all the beaches on Earth.

 Self-assessment Draw a star on three of your smoothest exit flicks.

Assessment: Exit flicks

Trace and then copy these letters with exit flicks.

a   a   d   d   m   m

n   n   u   u   i   i

t   t   h   h   k   k

v   v   w   w   o   o

Add exit flicks to the letters that need them.

Aurora   Earth   planets   galaxy

asteroid   gravity   Neptune

Self-assessment of exit flicks: Congratulations! You've learnt how to do exit flicks. Colour in your progress on page 3.

☐ I need more confidence   ☐ I understand but need practice   ☐ Over the Moon!

Passport

Teacher comment

Entry flicks

Introducing entry flicks

Learning intention:
To write letters with entry flicks

What is an entry flick?

Tip! Entry flicks appear at the start of some letters. This will help with cursive writing.

m → ᵐ entry flick / exit flick

Trace these letters with entry flicks.

i   j   p   m   n   r   u   v   w   x   y   z

Trace these letters and words with entry and exit flicks. Then add the letter to complete the word.

i i i	f__eld
j j j	ad__acent
p p p	Ne__tune
m m m	co__et
n n n	u__iverse
r r r	c__aters
u u u	Merc__ry
v v v	a__alanche
y y y	vo__ager

Practising entry flicks

Trace and then add entry flicks to the letters that need them.

a b c d e f g h i j k

l m n o p q r s

t u v w x y z

Trace these letters with entry and exit flicks, then write each one five times.

i   v

r   n

j   y

u   p

m   w

I am successful when I can:
- ❑ sit with my back straight
- ❑ hold the pencil correctly
- ❑ position my paper
- ❑ make my entry flick smooth rather than pointy.

What does an entry flick look like?

 Tip! Entry flicks are smooth and then lead to a point.

r

Trace and then copy the words below.

change   pattern   time   natural

human   actions   erosion   source

energy   axis   night   season

orbit   day   galaxy   dwarf planet

 Self-assessment Circle your neatest word and tick three of your best entry flicks.

Letters without entry flicks

Tip!

Capital letters do not have entry flicks because they don't join to other letters in the word.

Trace the text and add entry flicks to the letters that need them.

Alessia read a book from her school library that said: "In 1969, Neil Armstrong became the first astronaut to walk on the Moon". Then she taught her younger sister, Daniela, all the names of the planets in the solar system: Mercury, Venus, Earth, Mars, Jupiter, Saturn, Uranus and Neptune.

I am successful when I can:
- ☐ check my 3Ps
- ☐ make my entry flick smooth rather than pointy.

Consolidating

Learning intention:
To practise writing letters with entry flicks

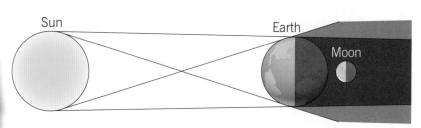

**The Earth rotates on its axis every
24 hours, which makes day and night.**

Trace and then copy the following text.

The Sun is a major source of energy that

warms our planet. It takes the Earth and

Moon 365 days (one year) to orbit the Sun.

Gravity from the Moon pulls on the Earth

and causes waves in the ocean.

Assessment: Entry flicks

Trace these letters with entry flicks then write each letter once.

i   j   p   m   n   r   u   v   y

Write four words that contain at least one entry flick.

Trace and then copy this text. Add entry and exit flicks to the letters that need them.

Ravi the astronaut flew to space in a rocket.

Self-assessment of entry flicks:

Congratulations! You've learnt how to do entry flicks. Colour in your progress on page 3.

❑ I need more confidence ❑ I understand but need practice ❑ Over the Moon!

Passport

Teacher comment

Diagonal joins

Introducing diagonal joins

Now you're ready to join some letters. Practise the diagonal join first. This join links the exit and entry flicks between letters.

Practise the diagonal join between h and i.

hi hi hi hi

Trace and then copy these diagonal joins.

ai   am   an   ap   ar   au   ay

ce   cu   cy   de   di   du   dy

en   em   ei   ey   he   hi   hu

ay   ce   di   ei   in   le   tr

Practising diagonal joins

Can you continue the pattern without lifting your pencil?

uuuuu uuuuu

uuuuu uuuuu

Circle your best pattern!

Trace and then copy these diagonal joins. The first one is done for you.

ie

| ie | im | in | ip | ir |

ie

| ke | ki | kn | kr | ky |

ke

| le | li | lm | lu | ly |

le

| me | mi | mm | mp | my |

me

ni

45°

The exit flicks go up at an angle of about 45 degrees to join to the next letter.

Trace and then copy.

ni ne nn nr nu ny

te ti tn tr tu ty

ue ui um un up uy

my tip in bin he her him

Diagonal joins to tall letters

Learning intention:
To use a diagonal join to tall letters

Without lifting the pencil, you can make a diagonal join with an extended exit flick.

a with an exit flick   a with a diagonal line up   a joined to h

a   *a*   *ah*

Trace these diagonal joins to tall letters, and then copy them below. The first one is done for you.

ah   ah   ah   ah   at   at   at   at

ah

ak   ak   ak   ak   ab   ab   ab   ab

ch   ch   ch   ck   ck   ck   da   da   da

Continue the pattern without lifting your pencil. Then go back and dot each letter i.

ilili   ilili

this ✓ *at* not this ✗ *at*

Trace and then copy on the lines below.

at at at at at at at

it it it it it it it

ut ut ut ut et et et et

Let's look at double letters, for example, double t.

Trace and then copy.

tt tt tt tt tt tt tt

Elliott Garrett Charlotte Odette Jett Yvette

Practising diagonal joins from q and z

The diagonal join from q to u is very long. Take the exit line from the q all the way to the top of the u.

Trace and then copy these letters.

q   q   q   q   q   q

qu   qu   qu   qu   qu   qu

Trace and then copy these words.

quiet   quiz   liquid   quest   quick   quasar

Give the bottom of the z a little wave before you do the diagonal join to the next letter.

z ← wave + diagonal join

Trace and then copy.

z   z   z   z   z

ze   zi   zy   zu   za

Trace and then copy these words.

zip   dizzy   lazy   dazzle

OXFORD UNIVERSITY PRESS

Consolidating

Trace and then copy the following text.

The book "Hidden Figures" is about three

African-American women, named Mary

Jackson, Katherine Johnson and Dorothy

Vaughan. These women were very smart and

worked hard. They overcame many obstacles to

contribute to the success of early space missions.

Assessment: Diagonal joins

Copy these diagonal joins.

ai   hu   ce   im   kn   zy   zi   qu

at

Show how these letters look when they are joined with diagonals. Remember not to lift your pencil! Use a coloured pencil to show the diagonal joins.

at   it   hi   hu   em   ie

ke   le   me   ni   ze

Copy these words with diagonal joins.

little   all   aunty   bike   they   then

Self-assessment of diagonal joins:

Congratulations! You have completed your diagonal joins. Colour in your progress on page 3.

 ❏ I need more confidence

 ❏ I understand but need practice

 ❏ Over the Moon!

Teacher comment

Passport

Drop-in joins

Introducing drop-in joins

Learning intention:
To write letters that contain a drop-in join: a, c, d, g, o and q

Tip! A drop-in join is used when we join to anti-clockwise letters. The exit flick from the first letter reaches high towards the top of the anti-clockwise letter. The anti-clockwise letter is dropped into place.

Trace and then copy these drop-in joins.

ma   ic   ed   ng   no   aq

ca   da   ea   ha   ia   la   na

ec   id   lc   uc   ad   dd   eq

Trace and then copy these words with drop-in joins.

quarter   lunar   giant   name

Practising drop-in joins

Tip! The dropped-in letter should touch the high exit as it moves down. Make sure there is no gap between them (retrace where necessary)!

Trace and then copy the dropped-in letters. In another colour, draw a star where the letters meet.

ag   dg   eg   lg   ng   ug   da

ag

co   ag   eg   ho   ig   to   mo

Trace and then copy these words with dropped-in letters.

again   magic   played   night

aqua   black   place   jumped

eight   equal   star   titan

OXFORD UNIVERSITY PRES

Joining to the new f

Learning intention: To write the new f with a head, body and tail

Tip! Remember, the new f has a head, body and tail. Make sure the f meets the exit flick of the other letter on the way down. When we join to the f, we drop in the letter f.

af

if

Trace and then copy.

af   af   af   ef   ef   ef

if   if   if   uf   uf   uf

often   lift   thief   after

chief   fifth   offer   nifty

Consolidating

Trace and then copy these drop-in joins.

Now you are ready to take off and write more connected words.

fifteen   tuft   beef   deft

wife   leaf   flag   cafe   benefit

refund   reflex   prefix   belief   define

Trace and then copy.

seat   fleet   gift   bench   screech

seal   site   star

titan   small

Join the dots to draw the Emu constellation, which is part of the Milky Way.

Assessment: Drop-in joins

I am successful when I can:
- ☐ check my 3Ps
- ☐ remember the new f has a head, body and tail
- ☐ connect my letters in words.

Trace and then copy.

dad   had   lad   mad   pad

big   dig   jig   pig   zigzag

Sirius   Buzz   Tuesday   left   right

helped   metre   system

Teacher comment

Self-assessment of drop-in joins:

Congratulations! You have completed your drop-in joins.
Colour in your progress on page 2.

Passport

- ☐ I need more confidence
- ☐ I understand but need practice
- ☐ Over the Moon!

Introducing horizontal joins

Tip! The letters o, r, v, w and x finish at the top of the letter, so we need to connect these letters with a horizontal join.

slight dip

on ri vu wi xi

Trace and then copy these horizontal joins.

oi   om   on   op   or   ou   ov   oy

ri   rm   rn   rp   rr   ru   rv   ry

vi   vu   vv   vy   vi   vu   vv   vy

Continue the fluency pattern.

vuvw   vuvw

Practising horizontal joins

Trace and then copy these horizontal joins.

ui   um   un   ur   wy   ui   ur

xi   xi   xp   xp   xu   xu   xy   xy

Copy these sentences. Then circle the words that contain a horizontal join.

George and Patrick love to study the

universe. This morning, they won an

award for writing

about asteroids.

The letters o, r, v, w and x only need a horizontal join (or exit flick) when they are joining another letter. They do not need an exit flick when they are the last letter in the word.

Horizontal joins to anti-clockwise letters

retrace section

ra

When making a horizontal join to an anti-clockwise letter, go across to the start of the letter, then retrace.

The orange line shows where the letter is retraced.

oa oc oo og os od

Trace and then copy these horizontal joins to anti-clockwise letters.

oa   oc   oo   og   os   od   oa   oc   oo

ra   rc   ro   rg   rs   rd   xa   xc   xo

wa   wc   wo   wg   ws   wd   va   vo

ocean   Saturday

Did you know that Saturday was named by the Romans after the planet Saturn?

The letter d is the only tall letter that does not start at the top. The horizontal join goes across to the starting point of the letter d.   *od*

Trace and then copy these words with horizontal joins to anti-clockwise letters.

Today   zoo   excited   rocket   wooden

revolve   garden   core   water

Trace these letters. Then, with a coloured pencil, shade in all the squares that have anti-clockwise letter pairs.

oo	tt	pl	xa	hi
ch	ss	og	ck	wr
rm	wo	se	go	os
op	od	fe	wa	ju

No, this is not me giving you a clue that there are 8 anti-clockwise letter pairs!

Write down your own anti-clockwise letter pairs.

Horizontal joins to tall letters

When you make a horizontal join to tall letters, go right to the top and then retrace a little as you move downwards.

above

on

below

Trace these joins to tall letters.

ot   *rt*   *rk*   *wb*   *uh*   *ok*

Trace and then copy.

ot   *ob*   *oh*   *ot*   *ok*

rt   *rk*   *rh*   *rb*   *wk*

wh   *wt*   *wb*   *xt*   *xh*

Trace and then copy these words.

chocolate   *girl*   *bark*   *stark*   *when*

woke   *solar*   *white*   *verbal*   *next*

Horizontal joins to f and t

Tip! For horizontal joins to f or t, swing up, then retrace on the way down. The crossbar on the f or t is just below the join.

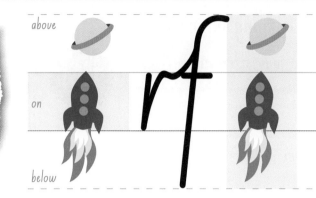

Trace and then copy the horizontal joins.

of   rf   wf   of   rf   wf

ot   rt   wt

ot   rt   wt

Trace and then copy the following words.

sort   surf   dwarf   of   part

robot   photo   teapot   other

Horizontal joins from f

Tip! For horizontal joins from f, use a straight line from the crossbar.

_fi fr_

Trace and then copy.

fi   fr   fu   fi   fr   fu   fl   fr

find   friend   from   flight   funny

When f joins to an a or o, you need to retrace a little.

_fa fo_

Trace and then copy these horizontal joins from f to anti-clockwise letters.

fo   fa   fo   fa   fo   fa   fo   fa

found   favourite   family   forty

Horizontal joins with double letters

Learning intention:
To write words with double letters

When we write double letters for r, o and f, we use a horizontal join. Make sure the double letters are not too far apart.

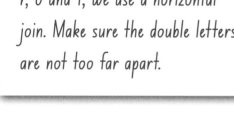

Trace and then copy.

rr   rr   oo   oo   ff   rr   rr   oo   oo   ff

rr   rr   oo   oo   ff   rr   rr   oo   oo   ff

Practise your cursive handwriting by tracing this sentence.

Sirius is efficient with his current

studies about outer space.

Consolidating

Learning intention:
To put my horizontal joins into practice

Trace and then copy.

My favourite friend is Faida. She often

comes to my house on a Sunday.

Once, we went to the park with my family

at night. We looked through a telescope and

saw the Moon. It was amazing!

Assessment: Horizontal joins

Copy these words with horizontal joins from o, r, v, w and x.

open   *town*   *axis*   *array*   *movie*

Copy these words with horizontal joins to anti-clockwise letters.

wait   *wrong*   *room*   *cosmic*   *rode*

Copy these words with horizontal joins to short and tall letters.

start   *pool*   *solar*   *crater*   *robot*

Copy these words with horizontal joins to and from f and t.

family   *football*   *fluff*   *roof*   *rotate*

Self-assessment of horizontal joins:

Congratulations! You have completed your horizontal joins. Colour in your progress on page 3.

❑ I need more confidence

❑ I understand but need practice

❑ Over the Moon!

Teacher comment

Passport

Letters that do not join

Learning intention:

To write letters that have clockwise finishers: b, g, j, p, s and y

Introducing clockwise finishers

Trace over the following letters. Draw a star ⭐ to show where the letter ends.
Draw an arrow to show the direction your pencil is heading in as you finish the letter.

b g j p s y

Tip! Letters that finish in a clockwise direction do not join.

Passport

Trace and then copy.

b g j p s y b g j p s y

be   best   bi   biggest   bo   boy

ba   back   bu   buying   bl   black

ge   get   gi   digital   go   gone

Practising clockwise finishers

Trace and then copy.

gh   bought   ju   just   jo   jobs

ja   jam   ji   jig   pa   past

pi   picture   pe   people   po   pole

pl   play   sa   said   sh   shopping

sl   slide   st   stayed   si   sister

so   some   yo   you   yu   yum

Capitals

Trace and then copy these names.

Ananya   Henry   Alessia   Moon   Binh

Emma   Sirius   Adam   Hoa   Ethan

South Pole   Nico   Charlie   Natalia

Answer these questions on the lines below.

In which month were you born?	In which country were you born?	On which planet were you born?

Draw an arrow on the world map to show where you were born.

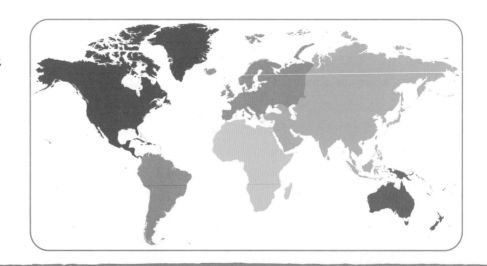

OXFORD UNIVERSITY PRE

Assessment: Letters that do not join

Capital letters do not join. Circle the letters that should be capitals, then rewrite the text correctly.

one night, juliette woke up and saw a

bright light shining in the sky. juliette

knew it wasn't the morning but then she

remembered her teacher telling her that

sirius is the brightest star in the night sky.

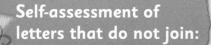

Teacher comment

Passport

Fluency and legibility

Learning intention:
To practise cursive handwriting

Practising cursive handwriting

Trace and then copy these sentences.

A star is a hot, glowing ball of gas. When

you look into the night sky, you can see

many shining stars. The light we see in the

daytime comes from the closest star: the Sun.

The Sun is approximately 150 million

kilometres from Earth.

OXFORD UNIVERSITY PRE

Rewrite the information in these fact files in cursive handwriting.

Mars is red and is the fourth planet from the Sun.

Neptune is blue and is the eighth planet from the Sun.

Saturn has rings and is the sixth planet from the Sun.

The Kuiper belt has asteroids and dwarf planets.

Kuiper belt

Do you know how to pronounce Kuiper? You say KIGH-puh.

Practising cursive handwriting

Size, slope and spacing

Rewrite the text, keeping in mind the size and slope of your writing. You may want to use the slope card at the back of this book. Place it behind the page you are writing on.

I'm Sirius.

Tip! Use your finger between words to make an even space.

The solar system is named after the Sun.

The word "sol" means sun in Latin.

All the planets in the solar system

revolve around the Sun.

Continue the fluency pattern.

uuu uuu

Numbers

Trace and then copy these numbers.

1   2   3   4   5   6   7   8   9   10

10 20 30 40 50 60 70 80 90 100

Write these numbers as words on each line. The first one is done for you.

11 eleven   eleven   eleven   eleven

12 twelve

15 fifteen

17 seventeen

18 eighteen

19 nineteen

20 twenty

21 twenty-one

Punctuation

Trace and then copy these punctuation marks and their names.

. . . *full stop* , , , *comma*

! ! ! *exclamation mark* ! ! !

? ? ? *question mark* ? ? ?

" " *speech marks*

Copy these sentences and choose the right punctuation mark to go at the end of each sentence.

Space travel is amazing

Do you have a favourite planet

OXFORD UNIVERSITY PRE

Labelling maps and diagrams

Complete the state and territory names on the map of Australia.

Tip! We use NSW Foundation Style print handwriting to label maps and diagrams.

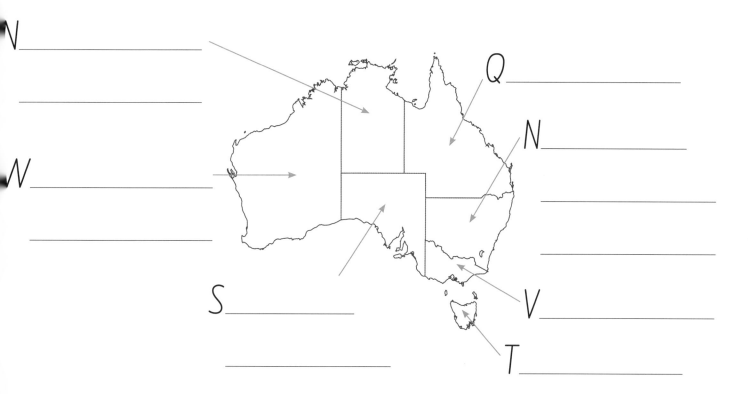

N_____

_____

N_____

_____

S_____

_____

Q_____

N_____

_____

_____

V_____

T_____

Label the planets in our solar system. Fill in the missing letters, using your knowledge from this book to help you.

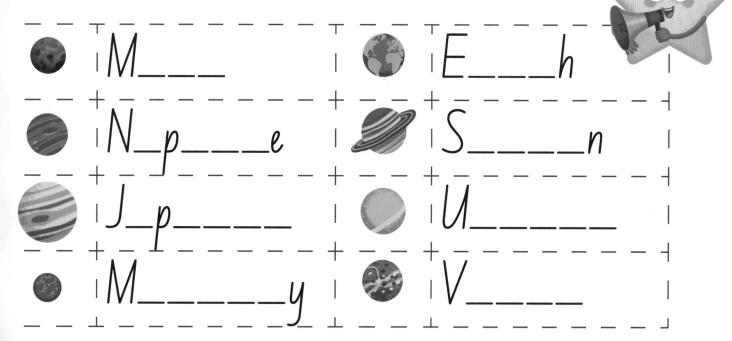

M____

N_p____e

J_p_____

M_____y

E___h

S_____n

U_____

V_____

Building fluency with high-frequency words

Practise writing these high-frequency words from the *Oxford Wordlist* three times each.

first

team

know

ride

time

amazing

fast

people

flying

watch

walking

awesome

beautiful

Word play

Complete the word search. Words can go upwards, downwards and across.
When you've found all the words, colour in the letters that are left over.

S	O	C	S	O	L	A	R	B	D	E	M	F
T	R	D	T	E	A	R	F	D	S	T	O	J
C	P	L	A	N	E	T	V	S	H	E	O	K
O	F	R	R	L	E	R	T	W	Q	S	N	Y
N	S	U	R	N	D	F	R	A	D	X	V	S
E	A	R	T	H	P	E	T	C	G	O	R	T
Q	T	R	I	N	G	S	Y	O	R	B	I	T
L	L	C	G	H	J	T	H	M	A	H	E	S
R	O	C	K	E	T	F	S	E	V	N	B	S
V	R	E	S	R	T	W	F	T	I	H	T	U
C	O	N	S	T	E	L	L	A	T	I	O	N
O	P	B	D	S	S	C	O	N	Y	R	I	N

olar   star   planet   constellation   gravity

rbit   Earth   Sun   Moon   rings   rocket   comet

Independent writing

Choose a planet to conduct some research on. On the next page, complete the fact file on your planet.

Print the name of your planet.

Draw your planet.

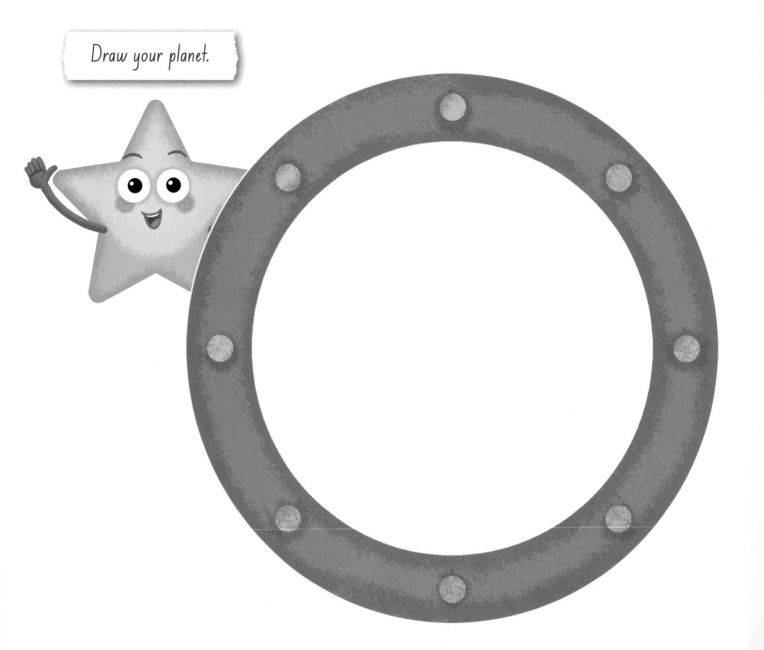

OXFORD UNIVERSITY PRE

My planet fact file

Assessment: Fluency and legibility

Copy these sentences in your best cursive handwriting.

 The biggest planet in the solar system

is Jupiter. Jupiter is twice as massive

as all the other planets combined.

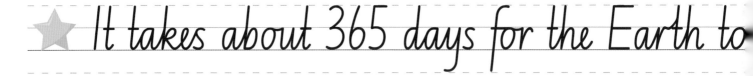 It takes about 365 days for the Earth to

complete an orbit of the Sun.

I hope you had fun and improved your writing on this journey.

Self-assessment of fluency and legibility:

Congratulations! You've learnt how to write legibly and with fluency. Go to page 3 to complete your passport.

 ❏ I need more confidence

 ❏ I understand but need practice

 ❏ Over the Moon!

Teacher comment

 Passpo